Are We There Yet ?

Great Car Games to Keep Families Sane!

Marks and Spencer p.l.c.
PO Box 3339
Chester CH99 9QS

shop online

www.marksandspencer.com

ISBN 978-1-84340-600-6
Printed in China

Are We There Yet ?

Great Car Games to Keep Families Sane!

Jo Pink

MARKS &
SPENCER

Contents

Introduction

Nobody likes long car journeys, especially children. Since becoming a mother, I've realised that your kids will soon let you know if they're bored; so on a long journey, various strategies have to be adopted to keep them entertained. And make sure you don't forget the perennial job of preventing them from going to sleep on each other, from picking small fights and car sickness.

Car games not only help solve the boredom of a long journey, but they can help to keep children's minds focused, so they don't fall sleep when you want them to stay awake.

In the 60s and 70s car journeys meant long hauls, uncomfortable roads and even less comfortable cars. During the summer months – when it used to get really hot and sticky – car journeys with bored kids were enough to drive anyone mad. Playing car games with my parents and brother made the trip pass that much quicker – my dad always refused to break any kind of speed limit, ever. A lot of the games you'll find in the book are the classic games that everybody played as a child (but may have been forgotten) while some I played as a child may have been unique to my family. Then there also are a few – like Bridge Baseball and Cow Football – that I've made up and then played on my own unsuspecting children to keep them happy.

I've tried to include games to cover almost every situation. Some of the games rely on busy roads with lots of vehicles around you; some are best played on empty country roads where you pass few vehicles; some are lively games; and some are designed to be quieter, calming games.

In the last few years the rise of in-car DVD players has helped to keep children entertained on the road, but they're far from a perfect solution. You end up leaving a house where the kids are hooked up to a screen, travelling in a car where they're hooked up to a screen, and then when you arrive at your destination they don't know what to do other than find another screen to watch. Car games are cheaper, far more interactive and let the children either entertain themselves, or involve others. Mostly though car games are just simple fun, designed to make you enjoy the time you spend couped up in a car together, rather than dread it.

Car games can test their imagination, too. I've included a number of easy word games that you can play together to help pass the time – whether it's in the car, on the train or waiting at an airport – helping to enrich your children's vocabulary en route.

So, let your car journeys become a voyage of discovery for every member of the family.

Jo Pink

Spotting Games

No matter where you go on a car journey, whether it's in the city, deep into the country or on a never-ending stretch of road, there's always a spotting game you can play. But you've got to be quick, because many of the objects are gone in the blink of an eye!

The Animal Game

For the animal game, you split the car into two halves. The right-hand side of the car takes the right side of the road, and the left-hand side of the car takes the left. This works well for a family of four, but it's up to parents how you split up three (or five) kids.

Whenever you spot animals in fields on your side of the road you have to count them out loud. So if you pass them too quickly, before you've got to fifteen – too bad!

The winner is the side who has counted the most animals. You can continue it in town, too, with domestic pets being walked or cats that dare to cross the street.

Variation

If you're passing through an area with few farm animals you can adapt it to any four-legged animals you see, provided you can shout out what they are. Try including animals you see on billboards – again their names must be shouted out loud to score points.

Instead of counting the animals out loud, you can make mooing, baaing or oinking noises. Great fun if there's more than one type of animal in the field!

So, What Am I Counting?

One player decides to count something outside. It could be street lights, telegraph poles, green signs, single-storey houses, ponds, dogs or roadkill. What they don't do is tell anyone what it is they're counting.

Instead, whenever they pass the object they've selected, they count out loud, adding to their score. The other players have to guess what it is that's being counted.

🚗 Playing Tip

To keep the game moving, ask players not to choose really rare things to spot – such as piebald horses, juggling sheep or houses with a ladder on the roof!

Variation
• • • • • • • • •

If the object a player has chosen doesn't appear within the next three miles then they lose their go.

Sequences

Number plates are a great source of game material as you'll find throughout the book.

Get players to choose their own number between 10 and 99 – such as 23 or 65 or 79.

Once everyone has chosen their number, they have to spot it on a number plate. If someone has the number 23 then BHT **523** wins, but BHT 253 is not close enough.

Variation
• • • • • • • • •

Players can try and get from 1–20 or 1–50, or have one team work up from 1 and one team work down from 20.

It's easy getting from 1–10, but from 11 onwards it gets tougher. This is also a good game for the whole car to play together.

Red Car!

A game that Henry Ford never imagined would happen (his famous motto was, "You can have any colour you like, providing it's black"). The Red Car game is simple. See who can spot a red car first. The person who spots it yells out, "Red car!" and gets a point. If they yell out "Red car!" and it's not, then it's minus a point.

Everyone has to see the red car for it to count.

Do maroon cars count? Yes
Do half-red cars count? Yes
Do red trucks count? No
Do cars with a red stripe count? It depends how big the stripe is.

🚗 Playing Tip
Darker colours are a nightmare to adjudicate

Variation
• • • • • • • • •

If you get bored of red, there's always blue, green, and yellow you can spot.

Special Number Plates

This number plate game sets players the task of finding different things when they scan their eyes across the road. You can play just for fun or give points each time someone spots one of the plates.

Words

Watch out for plates that spell out real words – no matter how short. There are endless three-letter examples, and quite a few short ones, too: IT, OR, OF, AS, AT, IS, TO, IF, US, UP, IN.

Remember, when playing for points, repeats aren't allowed!

Palindromes

Palindromes are words that can be read the same backwards, such as BOB or PIP. You can ask players to spot letter palindromes on number plates – they don't have to be real words – for example THT, GNG or LYL will score. Or you can try and spot number palindromes such as 121 or 848 or 999 or 2002.

Personalized Number Plates

There are a lot of personalized or "vanity" number plates on cars these days – registrations that spell out a word. See if you can spot one.

Variation
• • • • • • • • • •

You can play the games on this page singly, or you can combine them depending on how much traffic is around at the time.

Alphabet Sequences

This game is just like the number sequences game, except that instead of using number sequences the idea is to spot alphabet sequences. Again, it works best if the whole car plays as one team.

So, to start the game players need to spot the letter "A" on a number plate, then it's "**B**TY" or "**BC**M" or, if they're really lucky, "**BCD**" all on the same number plate.

However "**B**MC" would only count as the letter "B" (because the "B" and the "C" need to be close to each other — unless you want to play the game at lightning speed).

Variation
• • • • • • • • •

Split the car into two teams and have one team going backwards through the alphabet, from Z to A, while the other is working forwards, from A to Z. This works well as a race to finish spotting all the letters.

Dude, Where's My Orange Car?

If you want to give the kids something really difficult to do, ask them to spot an orange or a purple car. Orange may have been a big seller in the early 70s and 80s but ever since then cars in this colour have hardly been out of a dealer's showroom.

Variation

Or you could add Orange Car to a list of rare vehicles, such as:

Ice cream van
Vintage car
Tractor and trailer
Mobile crane
Boat on a transporter
Military vehicle

Glider in a trailer
Horse box
Road sweeper
Harvester
Motorcycle and
    sidecar

I Spy

A classic car game — one player secretly spots something on view to everyone in the car and then the other players have to guess what it is. For the very few that don't already know it, the person nominated starts by saying...

"I spy with my little eye, something beginning with S..."
The player who guesses correctly what that thing beginning with "S" is gets the next turn.

Playing Tip

Dedicated I Spy players will know that it's very easy to spot something outside of the car that all of a sudden gets left miles behind. So when the answer is finally uncovered there are cries of, "So where was that, then?"

To make sure everyone knows what the score is, best to get players to add if it's "inside" or "outside" of the car.

That way, if it's outside, players can look around straight away.

Cow Football!

Like the Animal Game the car is split into two teams and each team takes one side of the road. But we're talking American football for this game, not soccer.

Again the teams are looking out for farm animals: sheep, horses, pigs and cows.

The big difference is that this time the scoring system is based on US football scoring.

1–2 animals in a field = 2 points: Safety!
3–9 animals in a field = 3 points: Field Goal!
10+ animals in a field = 6 points: Touchdown!

Plus, the team gets an extra point after their touchdown – known as a Point After – if:

One of the animals is a completely different colour
One of them is lying down
One has a youngster suckling as you drive past.

For added reality, you can split the game into four 15-minute quarters.

Variation
• • • • • • • • •

The teams can impose a two minute Time Out if they suspect the car is about to drive past a big field of animals that will benefit their rivals. During the Time Out no points can be scored.

Time Outs cannot be called while you are driving past a field of animals, they must be called before.
Four Time Outs per journey; only one can be called in the last ten minutes.
Of course if you want all hell to break loose you can allow Time Outs to be taken mid-field, but expect some ructions from the backseat!

Glancing into the car, a policeman was astounded to see an old lady driving while knitting...

Realising that she was oblivious to his flashing lights and siren, the policeman wound down his window, turned on his loudspeaker and yelled, "Pull over!" "No", the lady yelled back, "It's a scarf!"

Danger, Aggressive Carrot!

Number Plate Phrases demands far more imagination than the other games.

Nominate a chooser to pick a passing car. They read out the number plate letters, such as DAC.

Then everybody has to instantly think of a three-word phrase or sentence starting with those three letters, such as: "Danger, Aggressive Carrot" or "Don't Argue, Caroline" or "Dogs And Cats".

The person who thinks up the best phrase gets a point.

Variation

The person who thinks up the phrase that makes the least sense is voted out.

Insist that nobody uses a name or that everybody has to use a name in their phrase.

That's My Car

A good game for a bunch of boys, or anyone who loves cars. This is also best played on a single carriageway.

Players pick a number from one to 100 — but preferably with at least 10 in between each player (to help build the suspense). Then together everyone counts the cars that pass in the opposite direction.

The number that each player chooses, that is the player's pretend car. When all players have found their pretend car, the player who "picked" the most impressive vehicle wins.

🚗 Playing Tip
Don't anything else except cars. If there's not much traffic on the road, count between one and 50. To avoid arguments over whose car is the winner, make sure an adult adjudicates.

Variation
• • • • • • • • •

Vary the game by picking a quality that is going to win. It could be the most luxurious car, the fastest car, the car that holds the most people, the cleanest car, the dirtiest car — you can make up whatever categories you like.

Bus Stop Battle

There are loads of ways you can play games with people standing at bus stops. Providing you're not travelling past them too quickly, or you're on the motorway.

Split the car into teams. One team takes the left side of the road, the other takes the right side of the road. Each time you pass a bus stop count the number of people waiting. The first team to reach 50 wins.

Variation

If you pass a bus stop with no one waiting then you delete one point from that team.

If there's an animal waiting at the bus stop they score 10 points.

Old ladies count two points — this can have everyone arguing so much that you can even miss bus stops. Some kids' idea of an old lady is anyone over 40!

What do you call a man with
a car on his head?
Jack

That's Your Dream Car, That Is

This isn't so much a game, more a way of poking fun at anyone in the car – especially the grown-ups.

The idea is to spot the most rickety old wreck on four wheels and say, "That's your dream car, that is!"

It doesn't have to stop at cars, it can be anything. For instance, if the car's passing a tumbledown old shack at the side of the road, someone could shout, "That's your dream house, that is!"

> **What did the jack say to the car?**
> "Can I give you a lift?"
>
> **Who drives away all of his customers?**
> A taxi driver!

The Traffic Light Game

In this simple game players have to guess how many traffic lights the car will go through on green before they get held up on red. All players guess at once and the person who gets closest to the right number wins.

Traffic Lights and Payphones is a much more involved game. Each player takes it in turn to own the car and tries to go through the most sets of traffic lights on green. If they hit a red light, their turn isn't always ended, as each payphone spotted between lights counteracts the next red. When a player runs out of payphones and hits a red light, their turn is over. The winner is the player who's passed the most traffic lights.

Variation
• • • • • • • • •

This game can be played by the whole car or individual players.

You can carry over payphones from one set of lights to the next. If there are few payphones around, then a church or religious building can substitute.

Two-doors versus Four-doors

This is a game for quiet, single lane carriageways – play it on a motorway and you've got yourself a sure-fire headache.

You can select any combination for this game, so divide the car into two teams (or choose two players) and decide what you're looking for. For example, one team counts the number of two-doors, vans, motorhome and lorries that pass by and one team counts four-doors, MPVs, pick-ups and motorbikes.

You can set a time or mileage limit with the speedometer, or, as in a lot of car games, a fed-up-with-this-game limit.

🚗 Playing Tip
You can assess the score as the game unfolds and do a little bit of levelling to keep things interesting. For instance, if four-doors are winning by a mile you can suddenly remember the rule that, "If a car is towing a caravan, boat, or trailer that's minus 10 points."

Bridge Baseball

Bridge Baseball is a great game to play on the motorway if you're passing through areas where there are few animals to count, but loads of bridges.

It helps a lot if you know the basic rules of baseball, but for those who don't, the aim is for a player to get round four bases before they get back home to score a point.

There's no stopping at a base and no pitching side, everybody bats. Once a player starts he has to keep on going.

The batting player waits for the first bridge to come along. If there is any form of human or four-legged animal life on the bridge, then they get to first base. The people can be in a car, on a bike, in a bus or crossing on foot, it doesn't matter which.

If there are no vehicles, or any sign of human life clearly crossing the bridge, that player is o-u-t, OUT! And the next player is in to bat.

The player at first base moves on to second base providing there's someone on bridge number two. Exactly the same rules apply, if something is either on or crossing the bridge they're in. If there's no one to be seen, they're out.

Tension rises after third base. Will they get to score...? Four bridges in a row with people, cars or animals crossing scores a point and then it's someone else's turn.

Treasure Hunt

The Treasure Hunt game needs a small amount of preparation before you set off on your journey. For each child construct a list of 10 things they have to spot on the journey. You can even incentivize them with a chocolate-for-objects-spotted scheme...

Each child has their own list and a pencil so they can cross off each item as they spot it through the trip.

The kind of things to watch out for will vary depending on what kind of countryside or urban landscape you're heading through. A mountain might be a good thing to spot if you are going skiing and a skyscraper might be handy if you're going on an inner city trip.

Here's some ideas of things you might include:

Fir tree	**Orange car**	**Burger King**
Dead tree	**Stripy car**	**McDonalds**
Fire engine	**Alsatian dog**	**Ford showroom**
Ambulance	**Traffic cone**	**Cinema**
Police patrol	**Digger**	**Theatre**
Bird of prey	**Railway bridge**	**Church**
Sheep	**Goods train**	**Castle**
Pig	**Passenger train**	**Hotel**
Horse	**Red bus**	**Billboard**
Pink car	**School bus**	**Petrol station**

Pub Cricket

First of all, you need a basic idea of what happens in cricket to play this game. Players take it in turns to be "in" or batting. Everyone then has to keep their eyes peeled for each pub that the car passes.

Most importantly they need to take a look at the pub sign to see how many legs are on it. For instance, if it's a pub called The White Horse, then it has four legs – and so the batsman scores four runs. If it's called The Coach and Horses, and there are two horses and a coachman in the picture, that's a total of 10 legs, so the batsman scores a massive 10 runs.

But if the picture has no legs – for example, The Crown, The Bell, or The Slug and Lettuce, they're out and it's the next player's turn.

When is a car driver not a car driver?
When he turns into a side road.

Did you hear the joke about the magic tractor?
It turned into a field.

Top Ten: Driving Songs

If boredom hits and the scenery is bleak, entertain each other with car-i-oke! Give your road trip soundtrack a topical mix by belting out a variety of car-themed tunes. Don't be afraid to sing your heart out and see if you can get other cars to join in! Here are 10 classic songs inspired by being on the road:

1. 'Drive My Car' – The Beatles
2. 'Cross Town Traffic' – Jimi Hendrix
3. 'Little Deuce Coupe' – Beach Boys
4. 'Greased Lightnin'' – John Travolta
5. 'Little Red Corvette' – Prince
6. 'Driving in My Car' – Madness
7. 'Drivin' South'– Jimi Hendrix Experience
8. 'Fast Car' – Tracy Chapman
9. 'Mustang Sally' – Wilson Pickett
10. 'Big Yellow Taxi' – Joni Mitchell

A policeman stopped a pedestrian who was trying to cross the road in a dangerous place. "You do know there's a zebra crossing just down the road!" he yelled at the man. "Really?" said the man. "I hope it's having better luck than me."

Guessing Games

When the landscape gets boring —
or maybe you're stuck on a plane
or at a train station — you can unleash
the power of imagination with a whole
variety of different guessing games.

Silent Counting

How long does a second last? The time it takes to say "one thousand" or even "one elephant?"

Here's the challenge. Ask someone in the car to count out a minute silently in their heads. At the same time, someone with a second hand on their watch keeps note of the time. When the player thinks they've reached a minute they shout out, "NOW!"

How many seconds are they off their target minute? Try it again with everyone in the car and see who can get closest.

Variation
• • • • • • • • •

Two, three or even four players can play this at once with everyone shouting out when they think the minute is up.

If you have three or more players give everyone a separate word, otherwise you won't know who's shouted out closest to the minute mark, whilst keeping your eyes glued to your watch!

Bing Who?
(or The Bing Game)

This is a game that splits the car in two – grown-ups versus children. And the grown-ups' decision is final.

The basic version of the game is as follows: the children in the car have to shout out a first name and the grown-ups have to think of a famous person with that name.

They can be celebs, sports stars, fictional characters from books, television and movies or even relations.

For every person the grown-ups name, they get a point – for every person they fail to name the children get a point.

Variation
• • • • • • • • •

Grown-ups, give yourselves five Time Outs for when the little rascals think up something fiendish, if you want to stack the odds in your favour.

Because the game requires a good knowledge of famous people, children are at a disadvantage in doing the naming, but they can always play among themselves if they are evenly matched.

Spoof

This game needs everyone to have three coins in their hand; they can be pennies, ten pence coins, whatever; their value is not important – they can even be non-sticky sweets.

You all put your hands behind your backs and secretly select whether you are going to keep zero, one, two, or three coins in the hand you put forwards.

With your other hand behind your back, present the hand with the coins, without revealing its contents. The aim of the game is to guess how many coins are hidden. This will depend on how many are playing. For example, if there are four people there could be a maximum of 12 coins and a minimum of zero.

One player starts off by estimating how many coins are hidden in total in all the hands. The first player calls out a number and everyone guesses a number in turn, making sure not to repeat someone else's number.

Once everyone has selected their number, the hands are revealed and the real number of coins is counted. The person who was closest to the total drops out. If it's a tie with two players, one number either side, then the round is null and void.

Play resumes, with the person to the left of the person who started in the first round, guessing first, until the ultimate loser is the last person in.

> **Which snakes are found on cars?**
> Windscreen vipers!
>
> **How can toads see on a darkened road?**
> They turn on their frog lights!

Variation

If you want to use the game as a way of getting your kids to learn to count money, you can count up the value of all the coins, and instead of asking everyone to guess the number of coins, guess the value of coins in each round.

With a smaller number of people in the circle use more coins to make things interesting.

What Am I?

A game very similar to Who Am I? but this time use things instead of people.

A player chooses a real-life object and the rest have to guess what it is by asking a series of questions for which the answer is either "yes" or "no".

Unlike the previous game, this version demands a much more detailed level of questioning, because "the thing" could be a bicycle, a hockey pitch, an aircraft carrier or a chicken nugget.

Variation
• • • • • • • •

Instead of choosing an object, choose an animal, fish, bird or insect. Or how about a plant of some kind? There is a similar sort of game known as Hidden In My Room. The first player secretly chooses an object then says, "Hidden in my room is something that is small..." or any adjective that describes the mystery object, such as "small", "furry", "smelly", or "black".

It would be a really lucky guess to hit on the right answer in one, so the players then get another chance when the chooser adds another description.

"Hidden in my room is something that is small and circular" and if no one guesses, the chooser keeps on adding clues until it is patently obvious what it is.

You can allow all sorts of things to be hidden in a bedroom that wouldn't normally fit, all the way from a tractor to a nuclear power station.

Who Am I?

Like Backseat Hide And Seek (see p.44), this game involves guesswork and asking the right questions.

One player chooses a person that they know, and that the other passengers in the car know. They don't reveal who it is.

Now it is up to the rest of the players to ask a series of questions that reveal their identity. All the choosing player must answer is "yes" or "no". So the interrogation could proceed along the lines of:

Is it a male? Yes
Is he Mum and Dad's age? Yes
Is he a teacher at school? No
Has he been to our house? Yes

There are bound to be a few questions that come up for which the chooser doesn't know the precise answer, so they can be allowed to give an approximate answer sometimes.

Variation

Branch out into pop stars, sports and movie stars, or even have a game based on cartoon characters.

Speed, Distance, Time

These games are all to do with the car journey.

Speed
Ask everyone in the car to close their eyes for 30 seconds (apart from the driver). Don't say what the game is going to be until everyone has their eyes well and truly shut. Then everyone has to use the sound and vibration from the car to work out how fast it's travelling. Guesses must be made before eyes are opened again.

Time
Make a note of what time you set off, then after you've gone half distance, ask everybody how long you've been travelling.

Distance
If you've zeroed the speedo before you start, at the same time as you're asking how long the journey's taken, you can ask how far you've travelled.

Or, spot a landmark on the horizon. Everyone has to guess how many miles it will be till you pass it.

Backseat Hide and Seek

Let's be honest, there aren't that many places to hide in the back seat of the car, especially when everyone has seatbelts on.

This version of Hide and Seek involves a lot more imagination than the real-life version. One player thinks of a good hiding place in their house or garden. The rest of the car has to find out where that is by asking a series of questions.

All the "hiding player" must answer is "yes" or "no". So the interrogation could proceed along the lines of:

Are you outside? No
Are you inside? Yes
Are you upstairs? Yes
Are you in the loft? No
Are you in the bathroom? No

The object of the game is to find the player with the fewest number of questions as possible.

🚗 Playing Tip

The player who's hiding has to find a place that is out of sight if someone were to walk into the room in real life. They can't be sitting at a desk or just standing to one side of the door.

They have to physically fit into the place described, give or take a few inches. Players can't get away with picking a place that only a small hamster would fit into.

A man was caught for speeding and went before the judge. The judge said, "What will you take: 30 days or £30?" The man thought about it for a minute and then replied, "I think I'll take the money."

Abstract Questions

It's a line of questioning you often see posed in magazine interviews when a celebrity is asked, "If you were a car, what kind of car would you be?"

It's usually meant to draw out a lighthearted or wacky response – for cars you can be fast and sporty, or you can be big and practical, or even luxurious and graceful.

Applying the same logic to a game, one player has to choose a person who they know very well. The other players must also know this person well and they have to guess who it is by asking a series of abstract questions.

For example:

If this person was a tree, what would it be?
If this person was an animal, what would it be?
If this person was a kind of weather, what would it be?
If this person was an emotion, what would it be?
If this person was a piece of clothing, what would it be?
If this person was a flavour of ice cream, what would it be?

Questions continue until someone guesses the right answer.

 Playing Tip

Before you start it's a good idea to limit your choices to a specific area, such as celebrities, athletes, fictional characters, people you know, etc.

To prevent the guessers getting sidetracked by misleading answers, the person answering can dodge the occasional question for which there is no obvious answer. Otherwise the guessers might be sent down a false trail.

To aid the guessers, the chooser can add clues into the answers.

The Next Car Will Be...

This is a game for wandering country roads, or winding mountain roads. Or just not very busy roads.

Players guess the colour of the next car to come past them in the opposite direction – white, green, grey, red, blue, etc. – everyone with their own separate colour. There's a point for each correct guess. Set a mileage on the car's speedometer to determine the finishing line.

Variation
• • • • • • • • •

Instead of using colours, you could pick types of vehicle that are going to come round the bend towards you.

Because cars are going to be the most common vehicles you can give higher points to other vehicles

Trucks: 2 points
Pick-ups: 2 points
MPVs: 3 points
Vans: 3 points

Motorbikes: 5 points
Car with trailer: 5 points
Tractor: 12 points
Police car: 20 points

Name That Beaten Out Tune

This one is a tried and tested favourite on car journeys. Instead of humming or playing a familiar TV theme tune, players have to beat out the tune against a car seat or anything that will make a noise: legs, containers but not a brother or sister!

Some that are normally recognized within 10 seconds:
The Muppets
The Simpsons
'Happy Birthday To You'
'Jingle Bells'
The National Anthem

Variation
• • • • • • • • •

You can try humming if the rhythm of the tune isn't a big enough clue.

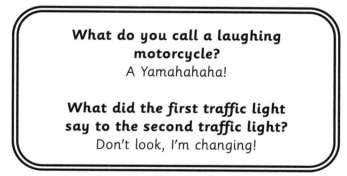 Playing Tip

With older children you can move on to films or even pop songs, but it's best not to try too wide a range of subjects or you'll be guessing all day, followed by the bitter accusations: "That didn't sound anything like (insert name of song here)" or, "I've never heard of that".

For the older, more complicated tunes, a clue or two might be necessary.

Keep the guessing down to a narrow field – such as cartoons, Disney film songs, No.1 hits, nursery rhymes etc.

What do you call a laughing motorcycle?
A Yamahahaha!

What did the first traffic light say to the second traffic light?
Don't look, I'm changing!

Top Ten:
The Car's the Star!

If you took these famous cars out of their hit movies or TV series then they just wouldn't be the same. Try naming the famous cars out loud and see if your passengers know what film or TV series they were from. There's a few in there for the car-mad dads too!

1. DeLorean – Back to the Future
2. Volkswagen Beetle – Herbie Goes Bananas
3. Ecto-1 – Ghostbusters
4. KITT – Knight Rider
5. Lightning McQueen – Cars
6. General Lee – Dukes of Hazzard
7. Batmobile – Batman
8. Ford Torneo – Starsky and Hutch
9. The Mystery Machine – Scooby Doo
10. Mach 5 Van – The A-Team

Top Ten:
Amazing Car Facts!

Unbelievable but true facts to tell the children – in case they are starting to get bored or fall asleep.

1. The New York City Police Department used bicycles to pursue speeding motorists in 1898.
2. In 1916, 55 per cent of the cars in the world were Model T Fords, a record that has never been beaten.
3. Most American car horns beep in the key of F.
4. The automobile is the most recycled consumer product in the world today.
5. An airbag takes only 40 milliseconds to inflate after an accident.
6. Mary Anderson patented the first windshield wiper in 1905.
7. On average a human being spends two weeks of their life waiting for traffic lights to change.
8. California has issued at least six driver's licenses to people named Jesus Christ.
9. The London motor show began in November 1895. The show consisted of five cars in a field, and only 500 people turned up.
10. The onboard computer in a modern car is more powerful than the one used to send the Apollo astronauts to the moon.

Action Games

It's time to sit up and pay attention; it's time for some action. These games involve waving and making hand shapes that will stir your children to life. All except one, which might just bring you some much-needed quiet – because it's an inaction game.

Rock, Paper, Scissors

Another classic game that can be played in the car, on the plane or wherever boredom strikes.

This is a game for two players who each make a sign with their hand at exactly the same time – either rock, paper or scissors.

Rock is a clenched fist, for paper, hold the palm open and flat and scissors is a closed palm with the index and middle finger forming a "V", like the open blades of a pair of scissors. Players keep their hand behind their back and then count, 1–2–3 and on 3, both players reveal which sign they have chosen, to see who wins the round.

Paper beats rock, because paper can wrap round rock. Rock beats scissors, because a rock will blunt a pair of scissors, and scissors beats paper, because scissors cut paper.

If players both choose the same sign it's a draw. Play as many rounds as you like.

🚗 Playing Tip
Make sure there aren't any last-second changes of hand signals.

Waving

It's fun to wave from the car when you're little. And people love to wave back.

A good game for a busy road, see how many waves you can get back in the space of half an hour.

Waving is good, smiling is great, but making faces is out. Especially if you're driving.

A game for the very young, you can get the kids to wave and teach them how to count (how many waves they get back) at the same time.

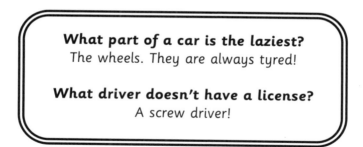

What part of a car is the laziest?
The wheels. They are always tyred!

What driver doesn't have a license?
A screw driver!

Waving Chicken

This is a game for long, empty roads with few cars about. It was told to me by someone who travelled a lot in Australia, where in the more remote parts, passing another car is a real event.

Because the most obvious "waver" is the person in the passenger seat, they have to wave on instruction from other people in the car. As another car approaches, a decision has to be made — do we wave or do we chicken out of waving?

If you wave and you get a wave back, that's a point. If you wave and you don't get a wave back, that's a minus point. If you decide not to wave and you don't get a wave, that's also a point.

But if you decide not to wave and the other car waves at you first, then that's the ultimate failure — two minus points!

The skill is working out what kind of car is coming towards you and whether the occupants of that kind of car are likely to wave or not.

🚗 Playing Tip
Don't try this on a motorway.

Noises

Whoever has hold of this book reads out a noise from the list below and the player has to name an object or animal that makes the noise. Or add some of your own favourite noise words to the list.

click	needeep	ding-	gurgle
eek	bong	dong	toot
splosh	crash	woof	hoot
tic-toc	ooze	miaow	parp
plop	squeak	tap	moo
boom	creak	woosh	honk
bang	slurp	ney	glug
click	bonk	bray	whistle
roar	crinkle	oink	whine
tweet	crackle	slurp	whinny
honk	rustle	tinkle	
clonk	rattle	slam	
clank	ding	splurge	

Invent your own points scoring system as to who made the most convincing, least convincing, loudest, quietest, most gruesome noise.

Expressions

If you have a potential actor or actress in the family, this is where they can take centre stage.

One person names an extreme emotion and one player has to make a face that expresses it.

Some good faces to act out are:

Happy	**Petrified**	**Loving**	**Thoughtful**
Ecstatic	**Grumpy**	**Sleepy**	**Intimidated**
Sad	**Angry**	**Sparky**	**Guilty**
Miserable	**Puzzled**	**Evil**	
Worried	**Suspicious**	**Goody-goody**	
Frightened	**Jealous**	**Disgusted**	

Variation

Get the person who chooses the emotion to whisper it in the actor's ear and then the other people in the car have to guess what it is.

Quietest in the Car

While a lot of the other car games challenge and excite the occupants of the back seats, this is one that calms everything down. This is often a great way to get younger children off to sleep. Our five-year-old daughter not only keeps very quiet, she also keeps very still and frequently drops off to sleep trying her hardest to win.

From the moment the signal is given everyone has to be as quiet as possible. The winner is the one who keeps quietest for the longest time.

These things are not allowed:

Humming
Coughing loudly
Distracting fellow competitors
Tickling other competitors

Playing Tip

If it's night time, make sure everyone's been to the bathroom, just in case of accidents...

Don't Laugh!

For this game players have to withstand all the efforts of the rest of the car to get them to laugh for one minute. They must keep a straight face throughout.

It's best if Mum or Dad can give it an unnecessarily long introduction. Something on the lines of: "Right, this is Isaac's turn at being absolutely silent. He's not going to laugh, giggle or even smile in the next minute. He's going to keep exactly the same expression on his face...and he's not going to say a single word, either. He's just going to look very, very serious."

Then when the clock starts, all the others can do what they like to try and get Isaac to laugh, without touching him.

Variation

Give the player with the "poker face" a nonsense phrase that they have to use as the answer to any question. For example, the answer he or she is given might be, "43 melons and a fly swatter".

The rest of the car then ask them questions, such as, "What are you sitting on?" to which the answer must always be, "43 melons and a fly swatter", said with a perfectly straight face. Just wait for it to crumple...

Mimes

There's more acting required in the mime game. One player has to act out an action, such as cleaning teeth, or sending an email, or taking a photograph, and the other players have to guess what it is.

Here are some ideas to get you going:

Cleaning shoes
Using the phone
Throwing a basketball
Putting on a coat
Painting a wall
Eating a banana

Using the microwave
Flying a kite
Writing a letter (don't forget the envelope and stamp)
Putting on sunglasses

Playing Tip
Start with very easy simple actions before moving on to the more difficult variations.

Variation

Be an animal – this one can have the car in fits of laughter (certainly my meerkat had such an uproarious reaction we had to stop the vehicle once, not because it was a great impression, either, the driver just couldn't stop laughing).

Without telling the rest of the car what they are, players have to mime popular, distinctive animals, from moles to meerkats, from kangaroos to koalas.

Importantly, players are not allowed to use any sound effects whatsoever. They can use their hands, for instance; to act out a cat licking its paws and cleaning its fur, or to show how big their ears are.

What happens when a frog's car breaks down?
It gets toad away!

What kind of ears do trains have?
Engineers (engine ears)!

Top Ten:
Songs For When You Are Lost

Sometimes when you find yourself lost and every sign post seems to be pointing you further and further from where you want to be it's easy for the family to get flustered. Make a playlist so that if you do get lost you have some music to calm everybody down. Here are some suggestions:

1. 'Take the Long Way Home' – Supertramp
2. 'Find the River' – R.E.M.
3. 'Can't Find My Way Home' – Blind Faith
4. 'On the Road to Find Out' – Cat Stevens
5. 'Lost and Found' – Eric Clapton
6. 'Searching' – Lynyrd Skynyrd
7. 'I'm Just Looking' – Dexy's Midnight Runners
8. 'On the Road Again' – Canned Heat
9. 'End of the Road' – Boys II Men
10. 'You'll Always Find Your Way Back Home' – Hannah Montana

As he was driving his old car down the motorway, the man's mobile phone rang. Answering, he heard his wife's voice urgently warning him, "I just heard on the radio that there's a car driving the wrong way. Please be careful!" "Its not just one car", he replied, "Its hundreds of them!"

Imagination Games

Involve older children with imagination games that challenge their story telling and descriptive powers. You'll never know how inventive they can be until you put them to the test. You can also find out if you have a budding drama queen in the family!

Don't Finish the Sentence

This game is sometimes known as the Never-ending Sentence. Players have to continue a sentence that someone else starts, but never quite bring it to a natural full stop.

Here's an example:
Player 1 ...I went to the doctor's on Friday, but...
Player 2 ...I couldn't find the right door to go in, so...
Player 3 ...I asked a man in the car park, who said...
Player 4 ...I'd probably come a day early and...
Player 1 ...it wasn't a good idea to...

The longer the sentence goes on, the more complicated and convoluted it becomes, but no matter how tempting, the players must never end the sentence.

And players are NOT allowed to leave the sentence hanging with the same linking word that others have used in the sentence.

The game ends when someone either duplicates a linking word or their words make no sense at all.

Happily Ever After...

Each player has to think up the ending to a made-up fairy story. The narrator starts off an improvised tale and builds up a few well-defined characters – knights, dragons, goblins, castles, princesses, witches, wizards, etc. – over the space of two or three minutes.

The story is paused with the characters in some kind of predicament. It's then the job of the other players in the car to try and provide the best ending which, as in all fairy stories, should have the hero and heroine living happily ever after.

Players vote to see which ending they think is the best.

Variation
● ● ● ● ● ● ● ● ●

For younger children, begin the story with characters they know from their own books and videos.

Of course it doesn't have to be fairy stories, but it's best to start off with a storytelling format that children are familiar with. From fairy stories, the wide world of literature is open to you. Just don't try War and Peace!

Car Poetry

Have a go at creating some car poetry on the move. If it's just five lines then you won't have to write the good ones down to remember them. One we created is published below.

Limericks are great fun and you can build them up slowly line by line. For example:

A beautiful princess called Hetty
Had fallen in love with spaghetti
She loved it so much
She loved even the touch
But the mess on her dress wasn't pretty

Each player can suggest a line of the limerick, or alternatively, build it up line by line together, agreeing which is the best next line as it is constructed, before moving onto the next one.

Variation

• • • • • • • •

A more artistic form of poetry can be Five-Senses Poetry or Five-Colour Poetry. With Five-Senses Poetry, each line is about a different sense — touch, sight, sound, smell, and taste, all relating to the same subject.

The sight of my dog makes me happy
The smell of my dog is so doggy
The touch of my dog is furry and wet
The sound of my dog is woof, woof woof
But the taste of my dog is NEVER!

With Five-Colour Poetry, each line is about a different colour.

A rose is as red as blood
The sea is as blue as my pyjamas
The grass is a green space I play on
The fire glows orangey bright
Dad's face is as black as a thunder cloud

Weird Vacations

Everyone can have fun planning a weird vacation with this nonsense game. Players have to make up a sentence about where they're going on holiday, who they're going with and what they're going to do when they get there. The only limiting factor is they all have to begin with the same letter.

The destination, the person (or thing) they're going with and their activity must begin with the same letter. For example:

I'm off to Paris with a parrot to pick poppies.
I'm off to Iceland with an iguana to idle about in an igloo.
I'm off to Zanzibar with Zoe to zoom around a zoo.

🚗 Playing Tip
If you allow names to be used, limit players to people they know in real life.

Just a Minute!

This is very similar to And They All Lived Happily Ever After, except this is a game for the whole car to play together. A narrator starts off a story and builds up a storyline for the rest of the players to follow.

It's then the job of all the players to take turns in developing the story for a minute before passing it over.

The story can go round and round getting more and more bizarre until the narrator decides to bring it to a close.

Variation
• • • • • • • •

Insist that each player has to kill off one character and introduce a new one in their minute of story-telling.

Or how about every player needing to include the same unusual word or phrase in their minute of storytelling — such as clogs, clarinet or cliff top?

So, What If...?

An imagination game, this one gives children the sense of what might be, what could be, if they think BIG enough.

So, what if you could have any superhero superpower?
What would it be?

So, what if you could load up a trolley in the toy store for free?
What three things would you pick?

So, what if you could go on holiday anywhere in the world?
Where would you go?

So, what if you could skip two lessons at school?
What subjects would they be?

So, what if you had a pop star put on a special concert for you and your friends?
Who would you choose?

So, what if you could have any pet?
What animal would you pick?

So, what if you could be a guest star in a top TV series?
Which one would it be?

So, what if your lottery numbers came up?
What would you spend your £10m on?

So, what if you could travel back in time?
How far would you go?

So, what if you could become invisible?
What would you do?

So, what if you could meet anyone from history?
Who would it be?

So, what if they made you a cartoon character?
Which series would you want to appear in?

What do monsters make with cars?
Traffic jam!

My Favourite Things

This is a game not played for points, but to find out what everybody likes about any subject imaginable.

Someone names a subject and each player in turn has to name their favourite; it could be anything.

To help you along here is a list of subjects:

animals	seasons	games	dances
car games	fast foods	shoes	hobbies
cereals	books	teachers	drinks
clothes	films	friends	toys
holidays	songs	jokes	smells
sports	pets	characters	shops
TV shows	flowers	names	pop stars

Variation
● ● ● ● ● ● ● ●

Bring in the "Yuck!" factor and get people to name their least favourite things. If you know each other well, try and guess what people's favourites are.

When I Went on Holiday...

This is a favourite old game that people know in many different forms. Basically, it's all about remembering a long list. Or, if you're bad at it, forgetting a short one.

A player starts with the sentence: **"When I went on holiday I remembered to pack...a toothbrush."**

The next player could add, for example, toothpaste. So they say: "When I went on holiday I remembered to pack a toothbrush and some toothpaste."

The next player adds another item to the list. "When I went on holiday I remembered to pack a toothbrush, some toothpaste, and my pet iguana called Alfonse." Gradually, the list grows until someone is bound to get the sequence wrong. And then they're out.

Variation
• • • • • • • • •

Personalize it with: Coming back from _____
I saw... And make players add things they really have seen or visited during the trip.

Top Ten:
Knock, Knock Jokes

Everybody loves Knock Knock jokes. Even the really bad ones can be funny and have the whole car in hysterics. Take it in turn and go around the car. Whose was the worst? Here are some of my favourites that I've picked up along the way. What are yours?

1. Knock knock
Who's there?
Albert
Albert who?
Albert you don't know who this is.

2. Knock knock
Who's there?
Ivor
Ivor who?
Ivor plane to catch so I can't stop long!

3. Knock knock
Who's there?
Aladdin
Aladdin who?
Aladdin the street's just pinched your bike!

4. Knock knock
Who's there?
Colleen
Colleen who?
Colleen all police vehicles in the area!

5. **Knock knock**
   Who's there?
   Eileen
   Eileen who?
   **Eileen'd on your car
   and dented it, sorry!**

6. **Knock knock**
   Who's there?
   Warner
   Warner who?
   **Warner lift, my car's
   outside!!**

7. **Knock knock**
   Who's there?
   Noah
   Noah who?
   **Noah good place
   where I can get my
   car fixed?**

8. **Knock knock**
   Who's there?
   Isobel
   Isobel who?
   **Isobel worth having
   on a bicycle?!**

9. **Knock knock**
   Who's there?
   Fred
   Fred who?
   **Fred you'll have to
   catch the bus 'cos
   I've got a flat tyre**

10. **Knock knock**
    Who's there?
    Wanda
    Wanda who?
    **Wanda buy a cheap
    car? It's got no
    wheels but...**

Word Games

Word up! You can re-invent car games
from many sources and some of these
games take their cue from TV, radio and
popular board games. The goal is always
to stretch everyone's vocabulary to the
limit while making it F.U.N.

The Nasty Butterfly...

This is less of a competitive game and more of an exercise in thinking up words and showing children the power of adjectives. The idea of the game is to think up two words you would never find written together, unless it was in some tall tale or nonsense poem.

Using words out of context can create fantastic, imagination-stretching word pictures. You can make boring words sound interesting or exciting words sound boring. It teaches children the fun — and power — they can have with words.

Boring Made Interesting
exploding headmaster
friendly wall
comfortable brick

Exciting Made Boring
lonely disco
miserable cartoon
sleepy roller-coaster

Animals Made Weird
hairy dolphin
sea-sick squid
intellectual ape

Objects Made Emotional
grumpy computer
sulky staircase
nervous ironing board

Opposites

A word game to challenge players' vocabulary and also their understanding of the meaning of words.

One person says a word, then the other has to find the antonym or opposite. Everyone starts with ten points and you lose a point for each time you can't find an opposite. The winner is the last one left in.

Happy/Sad
Brave/Cowardly
Strong/Weak
Loud/Quiet
Positive/Negative
Big/Small
Massive/Minute
Smelly/Odourless

Hard/Easy
Brilliant/Dull
Love/Hate
Narrow/Wide
Good/Bad
Ugly/Handsome
Tall/Short

🚗 Playing Tip
Don't let players get away with adding "un" on the front of words.

The Ticking Bomb

This game is another that requires a number plate to start it off. First, the chooser finds a plate with a letter sequence that is commonly found in a lot of different words.

For instance from the plate YEN 569 the chooser takes the letters EN. It's then the players' job to take it in turn to shout out a word with those two letters in, such as: Tent, When, Spend, Lend, Bend, Friend, Rent, Entertainment, etc.

If they can't think of something, it's up to the other players to count them down 5.....4....3...2..1–Bang! And the ticking bomb explodes.

That person then gets a point and at the end of the game the person with the least points wins. Anyone who repeats a word that's already been suggested loses the round and gets a point.

🚗 Playing Tip

This game can be shaped by whoever chooses the letters – so if younger players are involved, use simpler letter combinations and for older players, more difficult ones.

The Bong Game

This is a fun game to play over a short amount of time. One person in the car has to answer questions about themselves for a minute without saying no or yes. The second they say "no" or "yes" they're given the gong – Bong! – and they're out.

What's your name?
Michael
Your name's Michael is it?
That's right
You're nine?
Eight
Eight?
Yes
Bong!

Variation
● ● ● ● ● ● ● ●

Instead of banning the words "yes" or "no" you can nominate a different word. Make it a common word that crops up in a lot of sentences, such as "the", "and" or "but". Then ask someone a lot of questions, which they have to answer without using it.

🚗 Playing Tip

To make sure there's no cheating, you need to make sure that players stick strictly to the rules: Players must answer straight away, if they pause they can be bonged.

Players must answer correctly. If they shout out any old information in answer to the question then they can be bonged.

Players have to answer differently every time. They can't answer the same way twice. For instance, the older and smarter ones could try and use, "that's right" or "that's wrong" for "no" and "yes".

For an answer used twice they'll get the inevitable, "Bong!"

> **Why did the skeleton cross the road?**
> To go to the body shop!

Backwards Spelling

Another great game to teach word awareness. One player thinks of a word, then, without revealing what it is, begins to spell it out loud. Except they start with the last letter first and proceed to spell the word backwards.

The other players in the car have to work out what the word is going to be. The first person to guess and shout out correctly wins the next go.

So car becomes: R-A-C
Fun becomes: N-U-F
Cloud becomes: D-U-O-L-C
Games becomes: S-E-M-A-G

🚗 Playing Tip

Start with three- or four-letter words to get into the swing of things. To help players guess the words early, you can limit the subject area to particular themes – such as animals, plants or means of transport.

Compound Words and Phrases

This game is like a relay race for words with the baton being handed on each time. A compound word is a long word made out of two shorter words. Players have to form a word or phrase using the second word of a compound word or phrase.

A player starts with a word such as "Cargo" (car and go).

The next player has to find a word or phrase beginning with "Go".

So the sequence could progress:

Cargo–Go-Kart–Cartwheel–Wheelhouse–Housewife...

🚗 Playing Tip

Don't limit yourself to actual compound words or you're unlikely to get anywhere. Two-word phrases such as "Skipping rope" are fine.

Rhyming Bomb

Like the ticking bomb, players take it in turn to shout out a word that rhymes. This time though, it's not prompted by a number plate.

Someone starts with a word of their choice – for example, "Sally", this is followed by the others joining in with rhymes: "Rally", "Tally", "Pally", "Alley…"

Or perhaps: "Card", "Guard", "Shard", "Lard, "Hard", "Starred", "Sparred", "Barred".

If a player is stuck they get a 5-4-3-2-1 countdown before the explosion. The losing player gets to choose the next word that has to be rhymed.

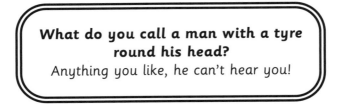

What do you call a man with a tyre round his head?
Anything you like, he can't hear you!

Verb and Noun Tennis

This game is based on words that are both nouns and verbs.

Players take it in turn to shout out a verb that is also a noun. So the sequence could go something like this:
Stamp–Load–Train–Log–Spell–Dive–Hop–Leap–Jump

The aim of the game is to keep a "rally" going as long as possible, and the more players in the circle, the more thinking time.

Variation
• • • • • • • • •

If you get really good at this game, you could even throw in an alphabetical sequence, so players have to think of a noun/verb with the letter "A" and then "B" and so on. Players can count forward the sequence of letters and anticipate what letter they'll be getting next.

The Janitor's Dog

The janitor's dog is an Awful dog.
The janitor's dog is an Awesome dog.
The janitor's dog is an Amiable dog.
The janitor's dog is an Aggressive dog.

For this game you have to find an adjective beginning with a certain letter. In this case we've used the letter "A", but it might just as well be the letter "C" or "D" (but probably not "X" or "Z").

Players take it in turn to find an adjective for the dog beginning with the letter "A", until someone repeats an adjective or gets stuck. That person is then out and the rest move on to another letter. The last person standing is the winner.

Variation
● ● ● ● ● ● ● ● ●

It's so easy to personalize this game. It doesn't have to be the janitor's dog or the farmer's horse; it could be your aunt's bathrobe or the mayor's tree.

Also, to make things a little more specific, you can choose positive adjectives or negative adjectives or even energetic adjectives.

Synonyms

For this game players have to find a group of words that all have the same sort of meaning – words that carry a similar meaning are called synonyms.

One player starts the game off by choosing a word such as "tired". The next player has to think of a word with a similar meaning, for example "fatigued", the next player might think up "weary" and the next decides on "exhausted".

Or the sequence could run: "shout", "yell", "scream", "roar", "cry", "howl", "bawl".

The game keeps on going until a player cannot think of one more word with a similar meaning, or they think of something that is not close enough. In this instance it could be words like "asleep" or "bored", which have a connection but don't really mean the same thing.

Lovers of Extreme Car Games could even bring their own mini Roget's Thesaurus with them.

🚗 Playing Tip
Keep the words as simple as you can to start off with.

Variation

To help the game along you can allow two-word phrases —
for our example it would be something like "puffed out" or
"worn out".

Alphabets

For this game players have to rack their brains for words on a particular theme. But they're not allowed to use just any words, they have to be words beginning with a certain letter of the alphabet.

Start the game off by naming a category. For instance:

Animals	Dogs	Jobs
Birds	Drinks	Names
Books	Fish	Rivers
Cars	Flowers	Song titles
Cartoons	Fruit	Sports
Cities	Furniture	Towns
Clothes	Games	TV shows
Countries	Films	Vegetables

Then someone else chooses the letter. Players take it in turns to name things from that category. Every time they think of something with the correct letter they put one finger (or thumb) up. If players can't think of something when it's their go, they drop out – and they're not allowed back in.

Colours

This is a straightforward game where players have to keep thinking up objects that are associated with a certain colour.

Either play as individuals, in sequence or all together, shouting the objects out.

Things that are green such as: grass, leaves, plants, hedges, gooseberries, apples.

Things that are black such as: coal, cats, dogs, tarmac, oil, police uniforms.

Things that are red such as: fires, autumn leaves, fire engines, strawberries.

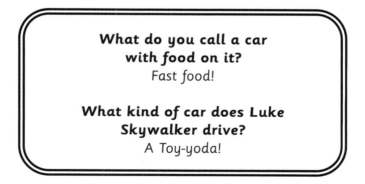

What do you call a car with food on it?
Fast food!

What kind of car does Luke Skywalker drive?
A Toy-yoda!

Letter Word Tag

You can play this game with all kinds of different word categories or themes. Someone decides the category, for example, "Geography". The first player picks a word such as "Caribbean" and then the second player has to name a geography-related word starting with the end letter of that word.

In this example it's the letter N, so it could be Namibia or Nova Scotia or Norway or New Orleans.

The following player has to quickly think up a destination beginning with the last letter of Namibia, and so on until someone becomes stuck and is bonged out. Start everyone off with ten points and deduct a point every time they get "bonged".

Variation
• • • • • • • • •

How about three-letter word tag and four-letter word tag, but on any subject you like.

For more themes or categories see Alphabets on page 98.

Rhyming Celebs

Rhyming slang is used by Londoners every day of the week and you can use it in a car game. Cockney rhyming slang substitutes a small phrase for a word, for example the phrase "mutt and jeff" means "deaf". This is a chance to make up your own rhyming slang.

Here are some more:
Apples and pears = stairs
Mince pies = eyes
Tom and Dick = sick
Dog and bone = phone
Pen and ink = stink

In this game, players invent a phrase, and the end word has to rhyme with a celebrity's name. The other players in the car have to work out who the celebrity is. For example: No need to push, it's...? The answer is George W. Bush.

She's got massive ears – it's Britney Spears
He's so scary – it's Jim Carrey
He's in the know – it's Russell Crowe
He likes a snooze – it's Tom Cruise
She loves her fiancé – it's Beyoncé

DropOut

This is a crafty word construction game that involves a bit of bluffing.

Like the never-ending sentence game, the idea is not to finish a word off. One player starts off with the first letter of a word, the second player adds a second letter, and so on – everyone who adds a letter must have an end word in mind, though they don't have to reveal it unless challenged. The letter they add mustn't complete a word.

For example:

Player 1: "H"

Player 2: "O" – they're thinking of the word "home"

Player 3: "S" – they're thinking of the word "host" (and "hos" isn't a word)

Player 4: "P" – they're thinking of the word "hospital" (and "hosp" isn't a word)

Player 1: "I" – they're thinking of the word "hospice or hospital" (and "hospi" isn't a word)

Player 2: "T" – they're thinking of the word "hospital" too and realize that Player 4 is going to get stuck with the last letter.

Player 3: "A" – they also realize that Player 4 is stuck with the word "hospital".

Player 4: "L" – they lose.

Player 4 collects the letter "D" for losing a round, the next time they lose it's the letter "R", then "O", then "P" until Player 4 becomes a DropOut and leaves the game.

If you add a letter you have to have an end word in mind. If the other players think that you don't they can challenge you. If you can't come up with an end word, then you receive a letter from DropOut. Alternatively, if someone challenges you about your end word and you have got a legitimate word in mind, then they collect a letter from DropOut.

Suffix This!

A suffix is an ending that is added to a word to form a derivative word. For example, "ment" is added to "commit" to form "commitment".

It can also be added to "state" to form a "statement". And when you come to think about it there are lots of "ment" words – arrangement, enlargement, agreement, and so on.

Go round the car in a circle, getting everyone to add a word to the list. There's no need to be editorially picky, it's supposed to be fun, so allow non-suffixes like "moment" or comment" to keep the game going.

Other endings to words you can try:

-ly	**-ant**
-tion	**-ingly**
-ent	**-ive**
-sion	**-ove**

Prefix That!

Instead of putting something at the end of a word, put something at the beginning – this is known as a prefix. For example "pre" can be added to the word "occupy" to form "preoccupy".

It can also be added to "mature" to form "premature" or form words like prepossess, preshrunk, prepaid, premarital, prehistoric and prejudge.

Other prefixes you can try:

Im-	Mis-
In-	Re-
Un-	Sub-
Dis-	Out-

Why did the cow cross the road?
To get to the udder side!

Why did the horse cross the road?
Because it was the chicken's day off!

A-Zs

Playing A-Zs is great for the car and is educational too. Each player takes it in turn to use the next letter of the alphabet to name a certain subject or object.

The great joy of this game is that you can make it as difficult as you want by choosing your subject accordingly.

Younger
Animals: aardvark, beaver, crocodile, dolphin, elephant, frog...
Girls' names: Anna, Britney, Chelsea, Diane, Ellie, Fay...
Boys' names: Ashley, Barnie, Charles, David, Edward, Finton...

Older
Trees: ash, beech, chestnut, Douglas fir, elm, fig...
Countries: America, Botswana, Chile, Denmark, Egypt, France...
Cars and car names: Aston Martin, BMW, Chrysler, Daewoo, Escort, Ford...

🚗 Playing Tip
**Set a time limit the bong out for the last five seconds – Bong, Bong, Bong, Bong, BONG!
Give players three "passes" so you can skip difficult letters.**

Fizz Buzz

Fizz Buzz is a game that can be played in the car, in airport departure lounges and it may eventually go off to college with them and get played late at night.

Players decide on a "Buzz Number" between zero and nine. Here, we'll make the buzz number three. Players have to count numbers out loud, going round in a circle, but they can't use the buzz number or its multiples.

Play would go like this:

Player 1: One   **Player 4: Four**
Player 2: Two   **Player 1: Five**
Player 3: Buzz   **Player 2: Buzz**

To add extra interest a "Fizz" number is thrown in. This has to be a different number—a good one to pick is five. So now the sequence goes:

Player 1: One   **Player 4: Four**
Player 2: Two   **Player 1: Fizz**
Player 3: Buzz   **Player 2: Buzz**

When it gets to numbers that are multiples of both – such as 15 and 30 and 45 – players have to shout out "Fizz Buzz!" If a player gets a number wrong they're out.

Signpost Lottery

There are hundreds of ways of playing signpost games and one of the easiest is Signpost Lottery. Apart from being a fun game it can also sharpen up everyone's mental arithmetic.

For this game you need to look out for roadsigns that give the mileage to various destinations.

If two players are playing, then one chooses to score every top-line mileage and one chooses to score every bottom-line mileage.

As the car passes a roadsign with mileage distances on, it's a battle to see whose mileage is the largest, top or bottom. For example:

Boston: 126
Cambridge: 84
Lille: 105

Top line mileage player wins by 21 miles, so his/her score moves to 21. Bottom line mileage player scores nothing.

If there is just one destination on the roadsign, then it's no score – because top mileage and bottom mileage are obviously the same!

> **Why did the dinosaur cross the road?**
> Because chickens hadn't evolved yet!

Variation
• • • • • • • • • •

Because roadsigns often have different numbers of towns and cities on them (anything from one to six destinations on a sign) the third player option is a complicated one. For this scenario it's a question of suck it and see. If you do have a third player who wants to get involved, they can score all the roadsigns where there is just one destination mileage. They can also score on roadsigns where there are three destination mileages and the middle one is the highest. (For four, five or six: tough luck!)

If your route has roadsigns that start with lowest mileage top and the highest mileage bottom – and many do – then swap around after each sign.

Similes and Anti-Similes

You can play around with similes in a number of ways. A simile is an expression that likens one thing to another. For example, cunning as a fox, stubborn as a mule, fit as a flea, mad as a hatter or hungry like a wolf.

One variety of the game is to play Guess The Simile. For this, a player thinks up a well-known simile and leaves out one of the elements, so the rest of the car has to guess the full expression: As _____ as a board. (The answer is stiff).
Or it could be done this way round: As old as the _____.
(The answer is hills).

Or you could play Anti-Similes. For this you have to substitute a rhyming word for the object of a well-known simile. Players take it in turns until they can't think of any more.

Here are some examples of anti-similes: as drunk as a punk, mad as a platter, I slept like a frog, he's as stubborn as a rule, to be strong as a box, cunning as some socks and helpless as a maybe (baby).

Alliteration

This is more of a comedy game for enjoyment than a game to score points in and win. Players have to produce a sentence using words starting with the same letter.

For example: Sally sucked a single sweet stupidly. Or: Timmy's train trundled through the tundra.

It's quite a hard task so you are allowed to use linking words, such as "and", "but", "while", "though", "if", "or" and "then" to keep the sentence going, as well as "the" and "a", but that's about all.

See how long you can keep going before bursting out laughing. Sometimes it's useful to have a pencil and paper to hand just to note down the very worst strangulations of the English language.

> ### What happened when the chicken slept under her car?
> She woke up oily next morning!

Top Ten:
Pioneers of Motoring!

When the car was first invented it changed how the whole world travelled. And it brought everybody who lived miles away that little bit nearer — even in-laws!

These facts are great for guessing games and, who knows, you may all end up learning something too!

1. The first car radio was invented in 1929.
2. The first cars had levers instead of steering wheels
3. The first car to be offered for sale was the Benz in 1887.
4. The first speeding ticket was issued in 1902.
5. The first ever grand prix motor race was held in France in 1906.
6. The first Monaco Grand Prix was in 1929.
7. The first fuel gauge appeared on cars in 1922. Up until then it was guesswork!
8. The American car maker Buick introduced the first electric turn signals in 1938 — up until then drivers had to signal with their hands.
9. The first ever land speed record was set on December 18 1898, when a French race car driver reached a dizzying speed of 39mph in an electric car.
10. The first self-propelled car was invented by Nicolas Cugnot in 1769.

What's the difference between a bus driver and a cold?
One knows the stops and the other stops the nose!

How do eels get around on the seabed?
They go by octobus!

General Knowledge

Learning is a lot more fun when you turn it into a game. You can harness a child's competitive streak to teach them lots of useful facts about the world around them – and we've included some funny and useless ones, too. Sometimes it's an education for the parents!

The Business Of Ferrets

There are some amazing collective nouns for animals. The word for a group of ferrets isn't a pack, posse or tribe – it's a "business" of ferrets.

This is a guessing game and you can use the list below over and over till you know them off by heart. You could even make up your own, such as a giggling of schoolgirls or a bunker of golfers.

Apes – a shrewdness of apes
Magpies – a tittering or a tiding of magpies
Elks – a gang of elks
Owls – a parliament or a stare of owls
Moles – a company, a labor, a movement or a mumble of moles
Ravens – an unkindness of ravens
Rook – a parliament, a clamor or a building of rooks
Bears – a sloth of bears
Caterpillars – an army of caterpillars
Woodpeckers – a descent of woodpeckers
Racoons – a nursery of racoons
Goldfinches – a charm of goldfinches

Hedgehogs – an array of hedgehogs
Pelicans – a pod or a scoop of pelicans
Eagles – a convocation of eagles
Peacocks – a muster of peacocks
Spiders – a cluster or a clutter spiders
Ibis – a crowd of ibis
Toads – a knab or a knot of toads
Monkeys – a troop of monkeys
Ducklings – a clutch of ducklings
Sandpipers – a fling of sandpipers
Ducks – a puddling, plump, raft or flush of ducks
Squirrels – a drey of squirrels
Turtle doves – a pitying of turtle doves
Tigers – an ambush of tigers
Guillemots – a bazaar of guillemots
Budgerigars – a chatter of budgerigars
Barracuda – a battery of barracuda
Pheasants – a brook or an ostentation of pheasants
Falcons – a cast of falcons
Crows – a murder of crows
Flamingoes – a flurry, regiment or skein of
flamingoes
Nightingales – a match, puddling or watch of
nightingales
Rhinoceros – a crash of rhinoceros
Leopards – a leap of leopards

Animal Families

When it comes to humans, it's man, woman and child. But do you know who makes up an animal family?

Badger – boar, sow, cub
Sheep – ram, ewe, lamb
Cow – bull, cow, calf
Cat – tomcat, queen, kitten
Deer – stag, doe, fawn
Dolphin – bull, cow, calf
Fox – dog-fox, vixen, cub
Goose – gander, goose, gosling
Pig – boar, sow, farrow
Mouse – buck, doe, kitten
Bird – cock, hen, chick
Bee – drone, queen/worker, larva
Horse – stallion, mare, foal
Lion – lion, lioness, cub
Leopard – leopard, leopardess, cub
Kangaroo – buck, doe, joey
Dog – dog, bitch, pup
Hare – buck, doe, leveret

Grasshopper – male, female, nymph
Goat – billy, nanny, kid
Elephant – bull, cow, calf
Duck – drake, duck, duckling
Donkey – jackass, jenny, foal
Dinosaur – bull, cow, hatchling/juvenile
Bear – boar, sow, cub
Alligator – bull, cow, hatchling
Otter – dog, bitch, whelp
Penguin – cock, hen, chick/fledgling
Possum – jack, jill, joey
Rabbit – buck, doe, kitten
Raccoon – boar, sow, cub
Termite – king, queen, nymph

Useless But True Animal Facts

The animal kingdom is full of strange creatures. Amuse yourself with these weird and wonderful facts, and maybe one day you'll experience them for yourself!

An **ant** can lift 50 times its own weight and always falls over on its right side when drunk.

All **polar bears** are left-handed.

A **snail** can sleep for three years.

The **flea** can jump 350 times its body length.

Turtles can breathe through their bottoms.

Butterflies taste with their feet.

An **ostrich's** eye is bigger than its brain.

Elephants are the only animals that can't jump.

Mosquito repellents don't repel. They hide you, so the mosquito doesn't know you're there.

Donkeys kill almost as many people every year as plane crashes.

Woodpeckers slam their heads into trees at a rate of 20 pecks per second.

It is possible to lead a **cow** upstairs...but not downstairs.

A **crocodile** cannot stick its tongue out.

Inventions

So how much does everyone know about the world's great inventors? You can ask questions on who invented what and what was invented when...

The **hot air balloon** was invented by...Jacques and Joseph
Montgolfier (France) in 1783.

The **ballpoint pen** was invented by...John Loud (USA) in 1888.

The **bicycle** was invented by...Kirk Macmillan (UK) in 1839.

The **car** was invented by...Nicolas Cugnot (France) in 1769, though it
was used as a tractor to pull guns.

The **cash register** was invented by...James Ritty (USA) in 1879.

Celluloid was invented by...Alexander Parks (UK) in 1861.

Cinematic film was invented by...Auguste and Louis Lumière
(France) in 1895.

The **CD** was invented by...Philips and Sony (Holland and Japan) in 1978.

The **electric lamp** was invented by...Thomas Edison (USA) in 1879.

The **gramophone** was invented by...Thomas Edison (USA) in 1878.

The **helicopter** was invented by... Etienne Oehmichen (France) in 1924.

The **hovercraft** was invented by...Sir Christopher Cockerell (UK) in 1952.

The **jet engine** was invented by...Sir Frank Whittle (UK) in 1937.

The **laser** was invented by...Dr. Charles H. Townes (USA) in 1960.

The **locomotive** was invented by...Richard Trevithick (UK) in 1804.

The **microphone** was invented by...Alexander Graham Bell (USA) in 1876.

The **motorcycle** was invented by...Gottlieb Daimler (Germany) in 1885.

The **neon lamp** was invented by...Georges Claude (France) in 1910.

Nylon was invented by...Dr. Wallace H. Carothers (USA) in 1937.

Photography on paper was invented by...W.H. Fox Talbot (UK) in 1835.

Photography on film was invented by...John Carbutt (USA) in 1888.

The **refrigerator** was invented by...James Harrison (UK) and Alexander Twining (USA) in 1850.

Rubber tires were invented by...Thomas Hancock (UK) in 1846.

The **safety pin** was invented by...Walter Hunt (USA) in 1849.

The **skyscraper** was invented by...William Le Baron Jenny (USA) in 1882, (a dizzying 10 floors).

Stainless steel was invented by...Harry Brearley (UK) in 1913.

The **submarine** was invented by...David Bushnell (USA) in 1776.

The **telegraph code** was invented by...Samuel B. Morse (USA) in 1837.

The **refractor telescope** was invented by...Hans Lippershey (Holland) in 1608.

The **television** was invented by...John Logie Baird (UK) in 1926.

The **thermometer** was invented by...Galileo Galilei (Italy) in 1593.

The **washing machine** (electric) was invented by...Hurley Machine Co. (Chicago, USA) in 1907.

The **water closet** was invented by...Sir John Harington (UK) in 1589.

The **zip fastener** was invented by Whitcomb L. Judson (USA) in 1891.

Capital Gains

A test of memory here: see how many capital cities from around the world your children know. It may even be a refresher for the grown-ups.

You can test individual players or let the children play as a team.

Afghanistan – Kabul

Algeria – Algiers

Argentina – Buenos Aires

Australia – Canberra

Austria – Vienna

Bangladesh – Dacca

Belgium – Brussels

Bolivia – La Paz

Bosnia and Herzegovina – Sarajevo

Brazil – Brasilia

Bulgaria – Sofia

Burma – Rangoon

Cambodia – Phnom Penh

Canada – Ottawa

Chile – Santiago

China – Beijing

Colombia – Bogota

Cuba – Havana

Czech Republic – Prague

Denmark – Copenhagen

Ecuador – Quito

Egypt – Cairo

Ethiopia – Addis Ababa

Finland – Helsinki

France – Paris

Germany – Berlin

Greece – Athens

Guyana – Georgetown

Hungary – Budapest

Iceland – Reykyavik

India – New Delhi

Indonesia – Jakarta

Iran – Tehran

Iraq – Baghdad

Ireland – Dublin

Israel – Jerusalem

Italy – Rome

Jamaica – Kingston
Japan – Tokyo
Jordan – Amman
Kenya – Nairobi
Kuwait – Kuwait City
Latvia – Riga
Lebanon – Beirut
Libya – Tripoli
Lithuania – Vilnius
Luxembourg – Luxembourg
Malaysia – Kuala Lumpur
Malta – Valletta
Mexico – Mexico City
Morocco – Rabat
Nepal – Kathmandu
Netherlands – Amsterdam
New Zealand – Wellington
Nigeria – Lagos
Norway – Oslo
Pakistan – Islamabad
Peru – Lima
Philippines – Manila
Poland – Warsaw
Portugal – Lisbon
Romania – Bucharest
Russia – Moscow
Saudi Arabia – Riyadh
Slovenia – Ljubljana
South Africa – Pretoria
South Korea – Seoul
Spain – Madrid
Sri Lanka – Colombo
Sudan – Khartoum
Sweden – Stockholm
Syria – Damascus
Thailand – Bangkok
Turkey – Ankara
U.K. – London
U.S.A. – Washington DC
Venezuela – Caracas
Vietnam – Hanoi
Zaire – Kinshasa
Zimbabwe – Harare

It's a Big, Big, Big World

It's quiz time now. Assembled here is a collection of the planet's vital statistics and a chance for you to see how much your children know about the world they live in.

The **biggest ocean** is...the Pacific, about 70m square miles (180m sq km).

The **second biggest ocean** is...the Atlantic, 41m square miles (106m sq km).

The **third biggest ocean** is...the Indian, almost 29m square miles (74m sq km).

The **deepest ocean trench** is...the Mariana Trench (West Pacific) 35,840ft (10,924m—so the oceans are deeper than the Earth's tallest mountain.

The **biggest desert** is...the Sahara, 3.25m square miles (8.4m sq km).

The **second biggest desert** is...the Australian Desert, 600,000 square miles (1.5m sq km).

The **third biggest desert** is...the Arabian Desert, 500,000 square miles (1.3m sq km).

The world's **tallest mountain** is...Mount Everest, which is 29,035 ft high (8,850m).

The world's **second tallest mountain** is...K2 (Chogori), which is 28,250ft high (8,610m).

The world's **third tallest mountain** is...Kangchenjunga in the Himalayas, which is 28,208 ft high (8,597m).

The **tallest mountain in North America** is...Mt. McKinley in Alaska, which is 20,320 ft high (6,194m) and was first climbed in 1912.

The **second tallest mountain in North America** is...Mt. Logan in Canada, which is 19,850 ft high (6,050m).

The **tallest mountain in South America** is...Cerro Aconcagua in Argentina, which is 22,834 ft high (6,960m).

The **tallest mountain in Africa** is...Mt. Kilimanjaro in Tanzania, which is 19,340 ft high (5,894m).

The **tallest mountain in Western Europe** is...Mont Blanc in France, which is 15,771 ft high (4,807m).

The world's **longest mountain range** is...the Cordillera de Los Andes in South America, which is 4,500 miles long (7,200km).

The world's **second longest mountain range** is...the Rocky Mountain range in the USA, which is 3,000 miles long (4,800km).

The world's **third longest mountain range** is...the Himalaya-Hindu Kush range, which is 2,400 miles long (3,800km).

The world's **tallest volcano** is...Ojos del Salado in Argentina/Chile, which is 22,588 ft high (6,885m).

The world's **deepest depression** is...the Dead Sea in Jordan/Israel, which is 1,296 ft (395m) below sea level.

The world's **longest glacier** is...the Lambert-Fisher Ice Passage in Antarctica, which is approximately 320 miles long (515km).

The world's **deepest cave** is...the Reseau du Foillis, in the French Alps, which is 4,773 ft deep (1,455m).

The world's **most extensive cave system** is...the Mammoth Cave system in Kentucky, which was linked with the Flint Ridge system in 1972 to make a combined length of 213 miles (345km).

The world's **longest river** is...the Nile, which is 4,145 miles long (6,670km). It flows from Burundi through Tanzania, Uganda, Sudan and Egypt to the Mediterranean.

The world's **second longest river** is...the Amazon, which is 4,007 miles long (6,448km). It flows from Peru through Colombia and Brazil to the Atlantic.

The world's **third longest river** is...the Mississippi, which is 3,710 miles long (5,970km). The source of the Mississippi is...Beaverhead County, Montana, USA. It encompasses the rivers, Mississippi, Missouri, Jefferson, Beaverhead and Red Rock. It is the longest river in one country and flows through Montana, North Dakota, South Dakota, Nebraska/Iowa, Missouri/Kansas, Illinois, Kentucky, Tennessee, Arkansas, Mississippi and Louisiana.

The world's **tallest waterfall** is...the Angel Waterfall on the Carrao river in Venezuela, which drops 3,212 ft (979m).

The **tallest waterfall in the USA** is...Silver Strand in the Yosemite National Park, California, which drops 1,170 ft (356m).

The world's **largest lake** is...the Caspian Sea in Iran/Kazahkstan, which covers 143,500 square miles (371,000 sq km).

Acknowledgements

Many of the games in the book have been handed down from generation to generation, no doubt ever since Henry Ford first started turning out large volumes of the Model T and the car became the transport of the masses. Some are derivations of games that started life in the home long before the advent of television, and some, such as Bridge Baseball and Cow Football, have been committed to paper for the first time in this book. I believe that the game of Rock, Paper, Scissors even started life in another culture. The Japanese play Janken-pon with choki (scissors), paa (paper) and guu (rock) to decide who goes first instead of tossing a coin.

So a big thank-you to all the original creators of the games, many of which, like Chinese whispers, have taken on their own form over the years.

Most of all I'd like to thank my children; Theo, Isaac and Hetty for unwittingly testing out all the games over the last ten years. The majority were played long before I had an idea to write this book, but their contribution has been invaluable.

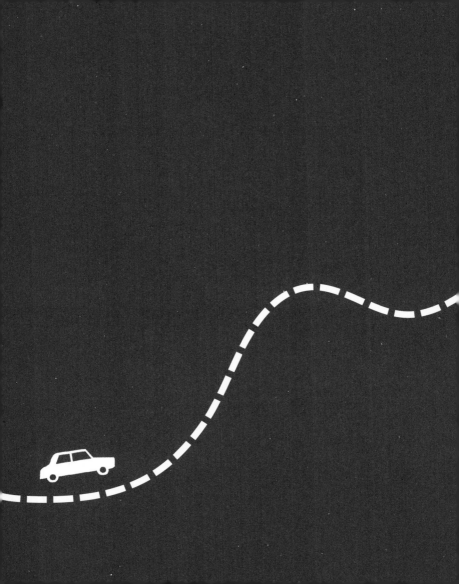